Finance 101 for the Glow-Up Generation

Secure the Bag with the Money Moves School Slept On

THOMAS GATSBY

FINANCE 101 FOR THE GLOW-UP GENERATION

COPYRIGHT 2024. ALL RIGHTS RESERVED.

No part of this publication may be reproduced, distributed, or transmitted by any means, including photocopying, recording, or other electronic or mechanical methods, without the prior written permission of the publisher, except in the case of brief quotations embodied in critical reviews and certain other noncommercial uses permitted by law.

Table of Contents

Introduction: Your Journey Begins Here	1
Chapter 1: The Wake-Up Call	4
Chapter 2: Goals Are Your GPS	6
Chapter 3: Money In, Money Out	8
Chapter 4: The Psychology of Money	11
Chapter 5: The Power of Saving	13
Chapter 6: Understanding Credit	14
Chapter 7: Demystifying Debt	16
Chapter 8: Banking Basics	17
Chapter 9: Investing Made Simple	19
Chapter 10: The Art of Diversification	21
Chapter 11: Retirement Might Seem Far, But...	22
Chapter 12: Navigating Market Ups and Downs	23
Chapter 13: The Necessity of Insurance	25
Chapter 14: Planning for the Unexpected	26
Chapter 15: Taxes—Maximizing Refunds and Minimizing Payments	27
Chapter 16: Buying Your First Car	29
Chapter 17: Housing—Renting vs. Buying	30
Chapter 18: Starting a Business	31
Chapter 19: Balancing Work and Life	33
Chapter 20: Building a Support Network	34
Chapter 21: The Role of Gratitude and Generosity	35
Conclusion: Own Your Financial Story	36
Glossary of Terms	37
Additional Resource	39

Introduction: Your Journey Begins Here

Imagine you're about to set off on the adventure of a lifetime—a cross-country road trip with your closest friends. The car is packed with snacks, the playlist is curated to perfection, and the open road stretches out before you like a promise. But there's one problem: you don't have a map or GPS. Without a plan, your epic journey could quickly turn into a series of wrong turns and dead ends.

Managing money is a lot like that road trip. You have dreams and destinations you want to reach—buying a car, traveling the world, starting a business—but without a financial roadmap, getting there can feel impossible.

Welcome to **"Finance 101 for the Glow-Up Generation."** This isn't your typical finance book filled with mind-numbing jargon and complicated charts. Nah, we're keeping it real and relatable. We're here to spill the tea on money matters that school didn't teach us but should have.

We'll follow the journey of Zoe, a 21-year-old navigating college life, part-time jobs, friendships, and her own aspirations. Through her story, we'll explore the ins and outs of personal finance in a way that's engaging, straightforward, and yes—even fun. So buckle up; it's time to take control of your financial destiny and embark on the glow-up journey you've been waiting for.

Part 1: Building Your Money Mindset

In Part 1, we meet Zoe at the beginning of her financial journey. Facing the reality of her dwindling bank account and impulsive spending habits, she experiences a wake-up call that many in the Glow-Up Generation can relate to. This section emphasizes the importance of setting clear financial goals as the foundation for financial success. Zoe learns to create SMART goals—Specific, Measurable, Achievable, Relevant, and Time-bound—that serve as her financial GPS.

She begins tracking her income and expenses, gaining insight into where her money is going. By understanding her spending patterns, Zoe identifies areas where she can cut back and redirect funds toward her goals. This part highlights the significance of cultivating a positive money mindset, acknowledging emotional spending triggers, and making intentional choices that align with one's financial objectives.

Chapter 1
The Wake-Up Call

Zoe sat in the back row of her Economics 101 class, doodling in the margins of her notebook. The professor's lecture on supply and demand blurred into background noise. She checked her phone under the desk—a habit she couldn't shake. A text from her bank app flashed on the screen: **Low Balance Alert: Your account balance is below $50.**

"Ugh, not again," she muttered, anxiety tightening her chest. She had just been paid last week from her part-time gig at the coffee shop. Where did it all go?

After class, Zoe headed to the campus café to grab a sandwich. At the register, she swiped her debit card. "Sorry, it's declined," the cashier said politely.

"Are you serious?" Zoe's face flushed as she fumbled for cash, coming up with only a few crumpled bills. She left the line, appetite gone, embarrassment lingering.

Back at her dorm, she sprawled on her bed and opened her banking app. The transactions told a sobering story:

- **$5.99** - Streaming subscription
- **$12.50** - Fast food
- **$29.99** - Online sale ("But it was 50% off!" she recalled)
- **$7.99** - Another streaming service
- **$15.00** - Ride-sharing service

The list went on. Small amounts that added up to a big problem.

Zoe sighed. "I can't keep living like this." She remembered her friend Malik, who always seemed to have his finances together. Maybe he could help.

That evening, she texted him: **"Hey, can we talk? I need some advice."**

Chapter 2
Goals Are Your GPS

The next day, Zoe met Malik at their favorite spot on campus—a quiet corner of the library overlooking the quad. Malik greeted her with a warm smile. "What's up?"

"I keep running out of money," Zoe admitted. "I don't understand where it all goes. I need to get my act together."

Malik nodded. "First step is knowing what you want. What are your goals?"

Zoe thought for a moment. "Well, I'd like to travel. I've always wanted to go to Japan. And I want to pay off my student loans sooner rather than later. Maybe start an online store for my art."

"Those are solid goals," Malik said. "Now let's make them SMART—Specific, Measurable, Achievable, Relevant, and Time-bound."

They spent the next hour breaking down her dreams into actionable steps:

- **Travel to Japan in two years:** Estimated cost $3,000. Save $125 per month.
- **Pay off $5,000 in student loans in three years:** Pay $140 per month.
- **Start an online art store in six months:** Need $500 initial investment.

"Wow, when you break it down like that, it feels doable," Zoe said, excitement creeping into her voice.

"Exactly," Malik replied. "Goals are your GPS. They give you direction."

Chapter 3
Money In, Money Out

Armed with her new goals, Zoe knew she needed to understand her spending habits. Malik suggested she track every expense for a month. "Think of it like keeping a food diary but for money," he joked.

She downloaded a budgeting app called **PocketGuard** and linked it to her bank accounts. At first, it was tedious to log every purchase, but soon it became second nature.

At the end of the month, the app generated a report:

- **Income:** $800 (coffee shop job + freelance design work)

- **Expenses:**
    - **Housing and Utilities:** $400
    - **Food:** $250
    - **Transportation:** $100
    - **Entertainment and Shopping:** $200
    - **Subscriptions:** $50
- **Leftover:** Negative balance

"Yikes," Zoe muttered. She realized she was overspending by dipping into her small savings each month.

She analyzed her expenses further:

- **Food:** Eating out accounted for 70% of her food budget.
- **Subscriptions:** She was paying for services she rarely used.
- **Entertainment and Shopping:** Impulse buys were killing her budget.

Zoe decided to make some changes:

- **Meal Prep:** Cook meals at home and limit eating out to once a week.

- **Subscription Audit:** Cancel unused services.

- **Shopping Ban:** Implement a 30-day rule—wait 30 days before making non-essential purchases.

By cutting $150 from her monthly expenses, she could start saving toward her goals.

Chapter 4
The Psychology of Money

Curious about why she had fallen into bad spending habits, Zoe did some research. She stumbled upon the concept of **emotional spending**—buying things to cope with feelings.

She reflected on times she shopped online after a bad day or treated herself to expensive coffee when stressed. "I've been using spending as a band-aid," she realized.

Zoe began practicing **mindfulness**, pausing to ask herself why she wanted to spend money on something. Was it a need or a temporary want?

She also started journaling, noting her moods and spending patterns. This awareness helped her make more intentional choices.

Part 2: Mastering the Basics

Part 2 delves into the fundamental principles of personal finance that everyone should know but are often overlooked. Zoe explores the power of saving by setting up automatic transfers to a high-yield savings account, building her emergency fund, and saving for her dream trip to Japan. She discovers the importance of understanding credit—how credit scores work, factors that affect them, and strategies to improve her score.

This section also covers managing debt wisely. Zoe confronts her student loans, learning about different repayment options and deciding to pay more than the minimum to reduce her debt faster. She examines her banking choices, switching to a bank that offers better terms and fewer fees. By mastering these basics, Zoe establishes a strong financial foundation that prepares her for more advanced financial endeavors.

Chapter 5
The Power of Saving

With her expenses under control, Zoe focused on saving. She opened a high-yield savings account online, which offered a 1.5% interest rate compared to her regular bank's 0.01%.

She set up automatic transfers of $200 from her checking to her savings account each month, aligning with her goal to save for Japan and build an emergency fund.

To make saving more engaging, she used a visual tracker—coloring in a chart each time she reached a $100 milestone. Seeing her progress visualized kept her motivated.

One day, her phone screen shattered. In the past, this would have been a crisis. But now, she had an emergency fund. She replaced her phone without stress, grateful for the safety net she'd built.

Chapter 6
Understanding Credit

Zoe realized she had little understanding of credit scores and how they affected her financial future. She knew Malik was savvy in this area, so she asked him to explain.

"Think of your credit score as your financial GPA," he said. "It tells lenders how trustworthy you are with borrowed money."

He broke down the factors influencing credit scores:

- **Payment History (35%):** Paying bills on time.
- **Credit Utilization (30%):** Using a small percentage of your available credit.
- **Length of Credit History (15%):** How long you've had credit accounts.
- **New Credit Inquiries (10%):** Too many can lower your score.
- **Credit Mix (10%):** A variety of credit types (loans, credit cards).

Zoe checked her credit score using a free app called **Credit Karma**. She had a score of 650—fair but with room for improvement.

To build her credit, she:

- **Paid Bills on Time:** Set up automatic payments to avoid missed due dates.

- **Kept Credit Utilization Low:** Used her credit card for small purchases and paid it off in full each month.

- **Avoided Unnecessary Credit Inquiries:** Didn't apply for multiple credit cards or loans at once.

Over the next six months, her score improved to 700. "Not bad," she thought, knowing a better score would help with future goals like renting a better apartment or getting a business loan.

Chapter 7
Demystifying Debt

Zoe's student loans weighed on her mind. She owed $5,000 with an interest rate of 4.5%. She wanted to pay it off quickly to save on interest.

She explored repayment strategies:

- **Standard Repayment Plan:** Fixed payments over 10 years.

- **Accelerated Payments:** Paying more than the minimum to reduce the principal faster.

- **Consolidation:** Combining multiple loans for a single payment (not applicable since she had only one loan).

She decided to pay $150 per month instead of the required $50, aiming to pay off the loan in just over three years and save on interest.

Understanding that not all debt is bad, Zoe also recognized the value of her student loan as an investment in her education.

Chapter 8
Banking Basics

Realizing she was paying unnecessary fees, Zoe evaluated her banking options. Her current bank charged monthly maintenance fees and ATM fees.

She researched and switched to an online bank that offered:

- **No Monthly Fees**
- **Free ATM Access**
- **Higher Interest Rates on Savings**

This change saved her over $100 a year. "Every bit counts," she thought.

Part 3: Growing Your Money

In Part 3, Zoe steps into the world of investing, demystifying concepts that often seem intimidating to newcomers. She attends workshops and uses beginner-friendly apps to start investing small amounts, understanding that even modest investments can grow significantly over time due to compound interest. The concept of diversification is introduced, teaching her to spread her investments across various assets to mitigate risk.

Zoe also begins contributing to a retirement account, recognizing the long-term benefits of starting early. She learns to navigate market fluctuations with patience and a long-term perspective, avoiding emotional reactions to short-term volatility. This part empowers readers with knowledge about growing wealth through informed investing and highlights the importance of planning for the future.

Chapter 9
Investing Made Simple

Investing still felt like uncharted territory. Zoe attended a free workshop at the community center titled **"Investing 101 for Beginners."**

The speaker explained:

- **Why Invest:** To grow wealth and outpace inflation.
- **Types of Investments:**
    - **Stocks:** Ownership in a company.
    - **Bonds:** Loans to a company or government.
    - **Mutual Funds/ETFs:** Baskets of stocks/bonds.

"Think of investing like planting a tree," he said. "The best time to plant was 20 years ago; the second-best time is now."

Motivated, Zoe started with a robo-advisor app called **Betterment**, investing $100 to start. The app created a diversified portfolio based on her risk tolerance.

FINANCE 101 FOR THE GLOW-UP GENERATION

Chapter 10
The Art of Diversification

Zoe learned that diversification was key to managing investment risk. Instead of putting all her money into one stock, she spread it across:

- **U.S. Stocks**
- **International Stocks**
- **Bonds**
- **Real Estate (through REITs)**

This mix helped cushion her portfolio against market volatility.

When a tech stock dipped, gains in other areas offset her losses. She began to see investing as a long-term game, not a get-rich-quick scheme.

Chapter 11
Retirement Might Seem Far, But...

Retirement felt like a lifetime away, but Malik emphasized the importance of starting early. He showed her the power of compound interest over time.

"By investing just $100 a month now, you could have over $150,000 by the time you're 65," he said.

Zoe opened a **Roth IRA**—an individual retirement account funded with post-tax dollars, meaning withdrawals in retirement are tax-free.

She set up automatic monthly contributions, viewing it as paying her future self.

Chapter 12
Navigating Market Ups and Downs

When the market experienced a downturn, Zoe panicked as her investment balance decreased. She considered pulling her money out.

She called Malik, who reminded her of the long-term perspective. "Market dips are normal," he said. "Historically, the market trends upward over time."

She held steady, and over the next few months, the market recovered. Zoe learned the importance of patience and not making emotional decisions with investments.

Part 4: Protecting Your Future

Part 4 focuses on safeguarding the financial progress Zoe has made. She encounters real-life scenarios that illustrate the necessity of insurance, such as unexpected health issues and car troubles. Zoe learns about different types of insurance—health, auto, renter's, and disability—and how they protect against unforeseen expenses that could otherwise derail her finances.

She also delves into planning for the unexpected through estate planning and understanding beneficiary designations. This section emphasizes that protecting one's financial future isn't just about accumulating wealth but also about mitigating risks and ensuring peace of mind.

Chapter 13
The Necessity of Insurance

An unexpected health issue landed Zoe in the emergency room. Without health insurance, the medical bills would have been overwhelming. Thankfully, she was covered under her parents' plan.

Realizing the importance of insurance, she also considered:

- **Renter's Insurance:** Protects personal belongings and provides liability coverage.
- **Disability Insurance:** Provides income if you're unable to work due to illness or injury.

She found a renter's insurance policy for $15 a month, giving her peace of mind.

Chapter 14
Planning for the Unexpected

Zoe's aunt passed away, leaving a small inheritance. It prompted her to think about estate planning, even though she was young.

She learned about:

- **Beneficiary Designations:** Ensuring assets go to the intended recipients.
- **Living Wills:** Outlining medical preferences if unable to make decisions.

While it felt heavy, she understood the importance of preparing for the unexpected.

Chapter 15
Taxes—Maximizing Refunds and Minimizing Payments

Tax season approached again. This time, Zoe was prepared. She:

- **Tracked Deductible Expenses:** Work-related costs, charitable donations, education expenses.

- **Used Tax Software:** Guided her through claiming credits like the **Lifetime Learning Credit** for her classes.

By being organized, she maximized her refund, which she invested toward her Japan trip.

Part 5: Navigating Life's Financial Milestones

In Part 5, Zoe faces significant life decisions that require careful financial consideration. She navigates purchasing her first car by researching and budgeting meticulously, ensuring the purchase aligns with her financial goals. The question of renting versus buying a home is explored, with Zoe weighing the pros and cons based on her current situation and plans.

She also starts her own online art business, applying the financial principles she's learned to launch and grow her venture successfully. This part illustrates how sound financial practices are essential when navigating major milestones and pursuing personal dreams.

Chapter 16
Buying Your First Car

With her old car becoming unreliable, Zoe needed a replacement. She researched extensively:

- **Determined Budget:** Based on her savings and what she could afford monthly.

- **Checked Loan Pre-Approvals:** To know her interest rates ahead of time.

- **Considered Total Cost of Ownership:** Insurance, maintenance, fuel efficiency.

At the dealership, she negotiated confidently, securing a good deal on a certified pre-owned car with low mileage.

Chapter 17
Housing—Renting vs. Buying

Zoe wondered if she should continue renting or consider buying a small condo. She weighed the pros and cons:

- **Renting Pros:** Flexibility, fewer responsibilities.
- **Renting Cons:** No equity building, rent can increase.
- **Buying Pros:** Building equity, stability.
- **Buying Cons:** Upfront costs, less flexibility.

After crunching the numbers, she decided to continue renting while saving for a down payment in the future.

Chapter 18
Starting a Business

With her finances in order, Zoe felt ready to launch her online art store. She:

- **Created a Business Plan:** Outlining goals, target market, and financial projections.

- **Registered Her Business:** Obtaining necessary licenses.

- **Invested in Marketing:** Utilizing social media platforms to promote her art.

Her store gained traction, and she began generating a modest income, reinvesting profits back into the business.

Part 6: Financial Wellness and You

The final part addresses the holistic aspect of financial health, recognizing that money management is closely linked to overall well-being. Zoe experiences burnout and learns to balance work, school, and personal life through effective time management and self-care practices. She builds a support network by connecting with like-minded individuals, fostering a sense of community and shared growth.

Practicing gratitude and generosity becomes a meaningful part of her journey, as she volunteers and donates to causes she cares about. This section underscores that financial wellness isn't solely about accumulating wealth but also about achieving a balanced, fulfilling life that aligns with one's values.

Chapter 19
Balancing Work and Life

As responsibilities grew, Zoe struggled to balance work, school, and her personal life. She felt burnout creeping in.

She implemented strategies to maintain balance:

- **Time Management:** Using planners and apps to schedule tasks.

- **Setting Boundaries:** Allocating specific times for work and relaxation.

- **Self-Care:** Prioritizing sleep, exercise, and hobbies.

By taking care of herself, she performed better in all areas of her life.

Chapter 20
Building a Support Network

Zoe realized the value of surrounding herself with like-minded individuals. She joined:

- **Financial Literacy Groups:** Connecting with peers focused on financial growth.

- **Entrepreneur Networks:** Sharing experiences and advice with other small business owners.

These communities provided encouragement, accountability, and resources.

Chapter 21
The Role of Gratitude and Generosity

Practicing gratitude, Zoe kept a journal, noting things she was thankful for each day. This shifted her mindset from scarcity to abundance.

She also continued volunteering and increased her charitable donations as her income grew.

Giving back not only helped others but enriched her own life, reinforcing the belief that wealth is not just about money but also about well-being and impact.

Own Your Financial Story

Standing atop Mount Takao in Japan, Zoe gazed at the breathtaking view. The journey to get here had been filled with challenges and growth. She had transformed her financial habits, achieved her goals, and set new ones for the future.

"What's next?" she thought with a smile. The possibilities felt endless.

Your financial story is yours to write. Like Zoe, you have the power to change your narrative, overcome obstacles, and achieve your dreams. It starts with a single decision to take control.

So, are you ready to embark on your own glow-up journey?

Thank you for joining Zoe on this adventure. Remember, financial empowerment is a journey, not a destination. Keep learning, stay resilient, and don't forget to enjoy the ride. Your glow-up awaits.

Glossary of Terms

A simple glossary explaining common financial terms used throughout the book:

- **Assets**: Resources with economic value owned by an individual or company.
- **Liabilities**: Financial debts or obligations owed to others.
- **Net Worth**: The difference between total assets and total liabilities.
- **Interest Rate**: The percentage charged on borrowed money or earned through investments.
- **Diversification**: Spreading investments across various assets to reduce risk.
- **Compound Interest**: Earning interest on both the initial principal and accumulated interest.
- **Credit Score**: A numerical expression of a person's creditworthiness.
- **Budget**: A plan for managing income and expenses over a set period.

- **Inflation**: The rate at which the general level of prices for goods and services rises.

- **Liquidity**: How quickly an asset can be converted into cash without affecting its market price.

FINANCE 101 FOR THE GLOW-UP GENERATION

Additional Resources

https://www.wtgpub.com/Finance101

SCAN FOR ONLINE LIST OF RESOURCES

Budget Templates

Downloadable Tools to Manage Your Finances:

- **Monthly Budget Planner**: A template to track income, fixed expenses (like rent and utilities), variable expenses (like groceries and entertainment), and savings goals.
    - *Where to Find:* Websites like Mint and EveryDollar offer free budgeting templates.
- **Expense Tracker Spreadsheet**: Helps monitor daily spending habits to identify areas where you can cut back.
    - *Where to Find:* Available on Google Sheets and Microsoft Excel Templates.
- **Savings Goal Worksheet**: Assists in setting and tracking progress toward specific financial goals.
    - *Where to Find:* Financial planning websites like Money Under 30 offer customizable worksheets.

Investment Platforms

Beginner-Friendly Apps and Websites:

- **Webull**: Commission-free trading platform for stocks, ETFs, and cryptocurrencies.
    - *Website:* wtgpub.com/links/webull
- **M1 Finance**: Invests your spare change automatically by rounding up purchases.
    - *Website:* wtgpub.com/links/m1finance
- **SOFI**: Offers fractional shares and personalized investment guidance.
    - *Website:* wtgpub.com/links/sofi

Educational Websites and Podcasts

Websites for Learning:

- **Investopedia**
    - *Description:* Comprehensive resource for financial terms, investing education, and market news.
    - *Website:* wtgpub.com/links/Investopedia
- **NerdWallet**
    - *Description:* Provides comparisons of financial products and tips for saving money.
    - *Website:* wtgpub.com/links/nerdwallet
- **Money Under 30**
    - *Description:* Focused on financial advice for young adults, covering debt reduction, saving, and investing.
    - *Website:* wtgpub.com/links/moneyunder30

Podcasts for Ongoing Learning:

- **"How to Money"**
    - *Description:* Hosted by two friends sharing practical money tips for everyday life.
    - *Listen:* wtgpub.com/links/howtomoney

- **"Afford Anything"**
    - *Description:* Explores how to make smarter decisions about money, time, and life.
    - *Listen:*
    - wtgpub.com/links/affordanything

- **"Planet Money"**
    - *Description:* NPR's podcast that makes economics accessible and entertaining.
    - *Listen:* wtgpub.com/links/planetmoney

- **"The Dave Ramsey Show"**
    - *Description:* Focuses on debt elimination and financial planning.
    - *Listen:* wtgpub.com/links/daveramseyshow

Budgeting and Financial Apps

Tools to Manage Money on the Go:

- **Mint**
    - *Features:* Tracks expenses, creates budgets, and monitors credit scores.
    - *Website:* wtgpub.com/links/mint
- **You Need a Budget (YNAB)**
    - *Features:* Encourages proactive budgeting and offers educational resources.
    - *Website:* wtgpub.com/links/ynab

- **PocketGuard**
    - *Features:* Shows how much spendable money you have after bills and savings.
    - *Website:* wtgpub.com/links/pocketguard

Books for Further Reading

Expand Your Financial Knowledge:

- **"Rich Dad Poor Dad" by Robert T. Kiyosaki**
    - *Synopsis:* Discusses the mindset and actions that differentiate the wealthy from the poor and middle class.
    - *Amazon:* wtgpub.com/links/richdadpoordad
- **"The Simple Path to Wealth" by JL Collins**
    - *Synopsis:* Offers straightforward advice on investing and achieving financial independence.
    - *Amazon:* wtgpub.com/links/simplepathtowealth

- **"I Will Teach You to Be Rich" by Ramit Sethi**
    - *Synopsis:* Provides a six-week program for managing money and building wealth.
    - *Amazon:* wtgpub.com/links/iwillteachyoutoberich
- **"Your Money or Your Life" by Vicki Robin and Joe Dominguez**
    - *Synopsis:* Explores the relationship between time, money, and personal fulfillment.
    - *Amazon:* wtgpub.com/links/yourmoneyoryourlife

Financial Tools and Calculators

Helpful Online Calculators:

- **Compound Interest Calculator**
    - *Purpose:* Calculates the future value of investments with compound interest.
    - *Website:* wtgpub.com/links/cicinvestor

- **Retirement Savings Calculator**
    - *Purpose:* Estimates how much you need to save for retirement goals.
    - *Website:* wtgpub.com/links/retirementcalculator

- **Loan Repayment Calculator**
    - *Purpose:* Helps plan repayment schedules for loans.
    - *Website:* wtgpub.com/links/loanrepaymentcalculator

Community and Support

Connect with Others on the Same Journey:

- **Reddit Personal Finance Community**
    - *Description:* A forum where you can ask questions and share experiences.
    - *Subreddit:* wtgpub.com/links/redditpersonalfinance
- **Facebook Groups**
    - *Examples:*
        - *"Budgeting and Savings Tips"*
        - *"Financial Independence for Millennials"*
- **Local Workshops and Seminars**
    - *Description:* Check with community centers, libraries, or local colleges for free or low-cost financial education events.

Government Resources

Trusted Information and Guidance:

- **MyMoney.gov**
  - *Description:* The U.S. government's website is dedicated to teaching all Americans the basics of financial education.
  - *Website:* wtgpub.com/links/mymoney
- **Federal Student Aid**
  - *Description:* Provides information on managing student loans and repayment options.
  - *Website:* wtgpub.com/links/federalstudentaid
- **Consumer Financial Protection Bureau (CFPB)**
  - *Description:* Offers resources to help consumers make informed financial decisions.
  - *Website:* wtgpub.com/links/consumerfinance

Career and Income Resources

Enhance Earning Potential:

- **LinkedIn Learning**
  - *Description:* Online courses to develop new skills.
  - *Website:* wtgpub.com/links/linkedinlearning
- **Coursera and edX**
  - *Description:* Platforms offering courses from universities on various subjects, including finance and business.
  - *Websites:*
    - wtgpub.com/links/coursea
    - wtgpub.com/links/edx
- **Gig Economy Platforms**
  - *Examples:* Upwork, Fiverr, TaskRabbit for side hustles.

Mental Health and Financial Wellness

Support for Financial Stress:

- **Financial Therapy Association**
    - *Description:* Connects you with professionals who address financial and emotional well-being.
    - *Website:* wtgpub.com/links/financialtherapyassociation
- **Mindfulness Apps**
    - *Examples:* Headspace, Calm for stress reduction techniques.
- **Non-Profit Credit Counseling**
    - *Description:* Organizations like NFCC offer free or low-cost credit counseling services.

These resources are designed to provide you with additional support and information as you continue to build your financial knowledge. Remember, the journey to financial wellness is a marathon, not a sprint. Utilize these tools to stay informed, motivated, and connected.

NOTE: Some of the sites list are affiliate links. I make a commission off them when you purchase, but it is at no additional cost to you.

Feel free to explore these resources and find the ones that best suit your needs. Good luck on your financial journey!

www.ingramcontent.com/pod-product-compliance
Lightning Source LLC
Chambersburg PA
CBHW030512220526
45464CB00006B/2758